MarketPlace	: AUS
Order Number	: 105-4795650-7749041
Ship Method	: Standard
Order Date	: 2013-01-02
Email	: rvxym96dtpht436@marketplace.amazon.com

Items : 1

Qty	Item	Locator
1	Midi Sequencing in C ISBN : 1558510451 R:	MUL-1-AL-07-043-25 LE

Mulberry House, Woods Way, Goring By Sea, West Sussex, BN12 4QY. Tel:+44(0)1903 507544
Email: international@worldofbooks.com | Twitter: @WorldofBooksltd | Web: www.worldofbooks.com

Beat	Quarter Note	8th Note	16th Note	32nd Note	64th Note	Triplets
		Ticks From Measure Start				
					412.5	
		420.0	420.0	420.0	420.0	
					427.5	
				435.0	435.0	440.0
					442.5	
			450.0	450.0	450.0	
					457.5	
				465.0	465.0	
					472.5	
5.0	480.0	480.0	480.0	480.0	480.0	480.0
					487.5	
				495.0	495.0	
					502.5	
			510.0	510.0	510.0	
					517.5	520.0
				525.0	525.0	
					532.5	
		540.0	540.0	540.0	540.0	
					547.5	
				555.0	555.0	560.0
					562.5	
			570.0	570.0	570.0	
					577.5	
				585.0	585.0	
					592.5	
6.0	600.0	600.0	600.0	600.0	600.0	600.0
					607.5	
				615.0	615.0	
					622.5	
			630.0	630.0	630.0	
				637.5	640.0	
				645.0	645.0	

	Quarter Note	8th Note	16th Note	32nd Note	64th Note	Triplets
Beat	**Ticks From Measure Start**					
					652.5	
		660.0	660.0	660.0	660.0	
					667.5	
				675.0	675.0	680.0
					682.5	
			690.0	690.0	690.0	
					697.5	
				705.0	705.0	
					712.5	

Note: The MPU-401 does not support fractional tick counts, so all fractional values have to be rounded. Any value shown here with a trailing decimal cannot be expressed exactly with the 120 ticks per beat resolution used by MT.

Appendix 2

MT Screen Messages

Messages are listed in alphabetical order.

All playback tracks are finished.

During the Record process on the RECORD menu you can keep record-ing after any tracks marked to PLAY have run out of data. When the last PLAY track is out of data, this message will appear at the bottom of the screen.

Already at most expanded scale possible, 1/1.

In the NLE screen you will get this message if you keep using the Ex-pand Scale command. The maximum expansion has one timing tick for every space the cross hair cursor advances. This means you can start and end notes with the maximum timing accuracy of 1/120 of a quarter note.

Be sure you run the program from the default drive.

If MT fails to find the .SCR screen files on the default drive/directory, you will get this message. Make sure that the .SCR files are on the same drive or hard disk directory as the MT.EXE program. Start MT from this drive/directory.

Could not allocate more memory(full?), record stopped.

During the Record process, memory is used up to save the MIDI data. If you run out of memory, you will get this message. Memory resident programs can eat up memory, so don't load them before running MT if you run into this problem.

`Could not open directory.`

MT checks that any drive/directory you specify in the DRIVE command exists before using it. In this case MT could not access the drive/directory. Check for typing errors. If you want to create a new directory for your song files, you will have to exit MT and use the MKDIR command to make the directory. MKDIR is documented in your DOS manual.

`Error in sending command xx hex. (repeat_cmd401)`

MT was unable to get the MPU-401 to accept a command. This probably means that the MPU-401 interface is not plugged in properly, or some other fault with the interface has occurred. For really stubborn problems, try shutting the computer off before trying MT again.

`Failed to load screen file.`

MT could not find all of the .SCR files on the default directory when starting up. Make sure you started MT from the default drive/directory and have all of the .SCR file in that spot. See Chapter 1 for a list of the needed files.

`First mark the START and END of the block.`

Both the START and END of a block of measures must be marked before you can use any of the block commands.

`Mark the start end end of the source block, then repeat.`

Block Repeat requires that the source block of measures be marked with Block Start and Block End before the Block Repeat is executed.

`Measure not selected, so block cancelled.`

If you move the cursor to a spot outside of the measure data area on MT's MLE screen and hit Return, MT will assume that you do not want to mark a block. An easier way to quit in the middle of any block command is to just hit the ESC key.

Memory pointer error in deleting note-off event.
Memory pointer error in deleting note-on event.

MT ran into some random data in the middle of the computer's memory. Possibly caused by a power flicker or a bad RAM chip. Reload the song file and start over.

No data-containing tracks have PLAY turned ON.

In the RECORD screen you must turn on at least one track to use the PLAY command. Move the cursor up to the PLAY row on a track that contains data and hit Return.

No track is active for recording.

In the RECORD screen you must turn on one active track before using the RECORD command. Move the cursor up the the RECRD row and hit Return. The word *ACTIVE* should appear for that track. You are now ready to record new MIDI data onto that track using the RECORD command.

Note OFF must be after note ON - No note added.

You tried to mark a Note Off before the Note On cross hair marker. Note Offs must be after Note Ons.

Source and destination measures cannot be the same.

You tried to copy a block onto itself. This is not allowed in MLE. If for some reason you really want to do this, you can copy the block to a blank track, mark that data, and then copy it back. Normally, you would transpose the block before copying it back.

The block must end at or after start.

You tried to mark a Block End before the Block Start. The End marker can be in the same measure as the Start marker, or in any measure after that on the same track.

The block must start and end on one track.

You tried to mark the Block End on a different track than the Block Start. They have to be on the same track.

There are no files matching _____.SNG on this drive/directory.

There were no .SNG files on the drive/directory specified using the DRIVE command on MT's primary menu. Make sure you have the correct drive/directory specified.

Unable to allocate more memory - Full?

Ran out of memory. If you have memory resident programs loaded, try rebooting the computer without loading them and restart MT.

Unable to reset MPU-401 - play process aborted.

MT was not able to get the MPU-401 MIDI interface to respond. Try shutting down the power to the system and then restarting. Check that your interface card and cables cables are fully inserted.

Unexpected clock out signal

MT unexpectedly was requested to send clock data to the MIDI OUT port. This is not a normal part of MT's operation. Perhaps the song file was corrupted.

Unexpected conductor data request.

MT unexpectedly got a request from the MPU-401 to supply conductor data. As supplied, MT does not allow you to change tempos within a song, so this request is ignored.

Ungetnext401 ran out of buffer space.

This means that MT got so much data from the MPU-401 that it was not able to process it. Probably noise on the MPU-401 channel. Check your connections and reboot.

Unrecognized data %x %x.

Some random data that MT could not interpret was received during the PLAY or RECORD process. MT keeps on working, but shows the data in hexadecimal just so that you know something odd happened.

Use arrow keys to move cursor, ret to select.

If you hit a letter or number key, MT looks for a command that begins with that letter. If there is a match, MT moves the cursor to that spot. If there is no match, you get this message.

You are already at the bottom of the MIDI scale.

You tried to move the NLE display below the bottom of the MIDI scale (5 octaves below Middle C). This is not allowed.

You are at the top of the MIDI scale already.

You tried to move the NLE display above the top of the MIDI scale (5 octaves above Middle C). This is not allowed.

You can only change meter if tracks are empty.

MT will not allow you to change the number of beats per measure if you have already recorded or loaded MIDI data.

You did not select an existing note.

The Delete Note command requires that you move the cross-shaped cursor to one of the notes on the screen in order to delete it.

Appendix 3

Function Finder List

File	Line No.	Function
mted2.c	203	*add_measure()
mtsc4.c	28	add_note()
mted2.c	386	*add_note_offs()
mted2.c	162	*advance_to_measure()
mtrc3.c	309	all_notes_off()
mted3.c	305	block_paste()
mted3.c	60	block_repeat()
mtsc2.c	134	*build_note_list()
mtrc3.c	285	calc_pct_free()
chain.c	46	*chain()
chain.c	88	*chainalloc()
mtrc4.c	200	change_channel()
mtsc4.c	246	change_vel()
mted3.c	220	clean_track()
videofnc.c	53	clearline()
videofnc.c	38	clearscreen()
mtrc4.c	373	clear_events()
mtrc4.c	335	clear_forward()
mtsc3.c	230	clear_select_lines()
mtrc3.c	247	count_events()
videofnc.c	71	csrplot()
mtrc4.c	295	data_dump()
chain.c	62	dechain()
mtsc3.c	27	*delete_note()
chain.c	77	dispchain()
mtsc1.c	208	display_keyboard()
filefunc.c	50	disp_files()

File	Line No.	Function
mtsc2.c	247	disp_notes()
videofnc.c	144	dotplot()
videofnc.c	182	drawline()
mtsc2.c	268	draw_note()
videofnc.c	158	draw_rectangle()
mted1.c	18	edit_menu()
mted3.c	18	empty_block()
mtrc3.c	193	erase_all()
mtrc3.c	174	erase_one()
mtrc3.c	148	erase_track()
mtrc4.c	27	*eventalloc()
chain.c	108	fdispchain()
filefunc.c	196	fget_from_file()
mted2.c	355	fill_note_array()
mted3.c	199	*find_event_before()
mtsc3.c	241	*find_note()
mtsc2.c	317	find_note_line()
filefunc.c	170	fput_to_file()
mtrc4.c	250	free_memory()
mtsc2.c	229	free_note_list()
writscrn.c	193	fwriteword()
mtrc4.c	81	get401()
mio401.asm	81	getdata()
filefunc.c	120	getdrive()
mtrc4.c	64	getnext401()
inputf.c	98	getstr()
filefunc.c	183	get_from_file()
inputf.c	115	get_string()
mtrc4.c	167	goto_measure()
mted2.c	83	has_midi_data()
mtut1.c	273	helpdisp()
mtut1.c	219	help_control()
mtut2.c	19	import_menu()
mted2.c	114	*increment_measure()
writscrn.c	165	initscrn()

File	Line No.	Function
mtrc3.c	81	init_401()
mtsc1.c	183	init_edit_param()
mted2.c	17	init_meas_data()
mted2.c	342	init_note_array()
mtrc3.c	271	init_rec_val()
mtsc2.c	27	init_screen_box()
mtrc4.c	222	init_tracks()
mtrc3.c	207	init_track_str()
chain.c	22	*inpchain()
filefunc.c	210	loadscrn()
mtut1.c	123	load_song()
filefunc.c	244	load_video_data()
mt.c	23	main()
mtsc2.c	300	mark_middle_c()
mtrc3.c	131	maybe_measure_number()
mted2.c	237	*merge_measure()
mtsc2.c	102	name_measure()
mtsc2.c	88	name_top_note()
mtsc3.c	263	note_to_float()
filefunc.c	25	pick_file()
mtrc2.c	21	play()
mtrc3.c	28	play_event()
mio401.asm	40	putcmd(n)
mio401.asm	105	putdata()
mtrc4.c	101	putdata401()
filefunc.c	157	put_to_file()
mtut1.c	176	recal_song()
mtrc2.c	102	record()
mtrc1.c	18	record_menu()
mtrc2.c	138	*record_track()
mtsc3.c	277	remove_event()
mtsc3.c	322	*remove_note()
mtrc4.c	139	repeat_cmd401()
mtut1.c	19	save_song()
mtut1.c	92	save_tracks()

File	Line No.	Function
mtsc1.c	18	scrn_edit_control()
mted2.c	136	select_measure()
mtsc3.c	71	*select_note()
mtrc4.c	110	sendcmd401()
videofnc.c	82	setvideomode()
mtut2.c	227	show_dest()
mtut2.c	213	show_source()
mtrc3.c	55	stop_401()
mtrc4.c	40	*store()
chain.c	96	*strsave()
mtrc3.c	325	trace_header()
mted3.c	142	transpose_block()
mtrc4.c	71	ungetnext401()
mtrc4.c	277	used_memory()
mtrc4.c	390	wait_for_key()
videofnc.c	199	wordul()
writscrn.c	142	writerr()
videofnc.c	22	writeword()
writscrn.c	221	write_int()
mtrc3.c	297	write_on_off()
videofnc.c	281	xsprite()

* Function names prefaced by an * return pointers. Files MTDECLAR.H and SCREENF.H contain full function prototypes.

Appendix 4

Microsoft and Turbo C Compiler Differences

With the exception of graphics functions, the Microsoft C compiler versions 5.0 and 5.1 are very similar to Turbo C version 2.0. Both support the ANSI standard for C syntax and libraries of functions. The only differences that crop up in MT's code have to do with which header file declares the library functions and non-standard functions that are specific to the IBM PC family of computers. This includes memory allocation in the *far* data heap and use of DOS functions for file service. These differences are handled in the source code by using the conditional compilation option supported by both compilers. For example:

```
/* #define TURBOC 1    Define if using TURBOC, leave
out for Microsoft */

#ifdef TURBOC
    #include <dir.h>
#else
    #include <dos.h>
#endif
```

If TURBOC is defined, the header file DIR.H is #included. Other wise DOS.H is used.

For large programs, the MAKE utility supplied with the compiler automates recompiling just the files that have been modified. The source code disk includes MAKE files for all programs that define TURBOC on the compiler command line for Turbo C:

```
tcc -mm -DTURBOC=1 mt.c                <- Turbo C version
```

The MAKE files for the Microsoft compiler do not define TURBOC on the command line:

```
cl /AM mt.c                        <- Microsoft C version
```

This allows the same program files to compile properly on either compiler without revision. If you plan to work with the source code using only one compiler, just delete the lines that refer to the alternate compiler and forget about the TURBOC defined word.

Graphics functions are another matter. Microsoft and Turbo C's approaches to graphics are completely different. This is understandable, as graphics are not part of the ANSI standard for C.

Microsoft implements graphics with a straightforward set of basic graphics functions. These are library functions, which are included at link time to form the finished program. The functions support CGA, EGA and VGA graphics modes, but not the Hercules monochrome graphics mode. Microsoft's text output functions work through the BIOS and are slow. This is circumvented in MT with the direct-to-video-RAM function *fwriteword()* defined in WRITSCRN.C. The slower library functions have the property of working in both text and graphics modes, so these are also used by the MT program, primarily in the NLE graphics screen.

The virtue of Microsoft's implementation of graphics is that the functions are small, portable, and easy to use. The drawbacks are the lack of flexibility and power.

The Turbo C graphics library is more elaborate. Graphics drivers are provided as separate .BGI files that are normally not included until the program is running and accesses a graphics mode. This allows programs like MT, which use mostly text modes, to not load graphics routines unless needed. This saves memory for larger song files.

By using separate drivers, Turbo C provides support for a wide range of video equipment including AT&T and Hercules graphics.Using the default "load when needed" mode, the graphics driver file must be available to the program when a graphics mode is initialized. Turbo C also supports converting the .BGI files into .OBJ files that can be linked into the finished program. This requires adding each driver that will potentially be needed by the end user. This eliminates the need to have the .BGI files on the drive/directory with MT.

Turbo C's text display functions default to writing directly to the video RAM area. This much faster than going through the BIOS, but not as portable. The text functions can be forced to use the BIOS routines by defining the variable *directvideo* to be zero. This is how MT writes characters to the graphics screen.

Turbo C also includes functions for detecting what type of video equipment is being used, for displaying text on the graphics screen with different fonts and font sizes, and a host of well thought out graphics shape displays. Unfortunately, no counterpart to many of these exists in the Microsoft library.

By design, the MT source code must compile on both the Microsoft and Turbo C compilers. This required holding back Turbo C graphics possibilities to maintain compatibility with Microsoft's library. To minimize the disruption from graphics differences, all compiler specific graphic functions are concentrated in the file VIDEOFNC.C. The TURBOC define word is used to separate the Microsoft from Turbo functions.

In the text modes MT uses the C coded *fwriteword()* function for fast direct-to-RAM screen writing. In the graphics modes MT uses the BIOS character writing routines. The limited amount of text on the NLE screen makes this practical. With Microsoft's BIOS library, text writing to the screen works well in all modes. Turbo C's library does fine, except when a graphics screen has more than twenty-five logical character lines. After line 25, the Turbo C functions fail. This means that Turbo C will not support character writing to the bottom of the high-resolution VGA screen. VGA emulation of CGA and EGA modes works fine. Other, more sophisticated functions are provided in the Turbo C library which works fine in VGA modes, but these do not have equivalents in the Microsoft library and could not be used in MT.

The ready-to-run version of MT on the program disk was compiled with the Microsoft C compiler. CGA, EGA, and VGA modes all work fine, but Hercules graphics are not possible. You can recompile using Turbo C to use Turbo's graphics libraries. This allows use of Hercules graphics, but runs into the BIOS problem with VGA modes using more than twenty-five character lines. This limits MT to mode 16 and below. This limit can in turn be overcome by using the Turbo C graphics functions like *outtextxy()*, but at the cost of losing Microsoft compiler compatibility. If you are using Turbo C, you may not care about Microsoft library limits, so many improvements are possible.

Appendix 5

MIDI 1.0 Detail Specification Tables

The following tables are reprinted from pages 9–18 of the *MIDI 1.0 Detail Specification*, courtesy of the International MIDI Association.

TABLE I

SUMMARY OF STATUS BYTES

Hex	STATUS Binary D7--D0		NUMBER OF DATA BYTES	DESCRIPTION
Channel Voice Messages				
8nH	1000nnnn		2	Note Off
9nH	1001nnnn		2	Note On (a velocity of 0 = Note Off)
AnH	1010nnnn		2	Polyphonic key pressure/Aftertouch
BnH	1011nnnn		2	Control change
CnH	1100nnnn		1	Program change
DnH	1101nnnn		1	Channel pressure/After touch
EnH	1110nnnn		2	Pitch bend change
Channel Mode Messages				
BnH	1011nnnn	(01111xxx)	2	Selects Channel Mode
System Messages				
F0H	11110000		*****	System Exclusive
	11110sss		0 to 2	System Common
	11111ttt		0	System Real Time

NOTES:

nnnn:	N-1, where N = Channel #, i.e. 0000 is Channel 1, 0001 is Channel 2, and 1111 is Channel 16.
*****:	0iiiiiii, data, ..., EOX
iiiiiii:	Identification
sss:	1 to 7
ttt:	0 to 7
xxx:	Channel Mode messages are sent under the same Status Byte as the Control Change messages (BnH). They are differentiated by the first data byte which will have a value from 121 to 127 for Channel Mode messages.

TABLE II

CHANNEL VOICE MESSAGES

STATUS		DATA BYTES	DESCRIPTION
Hex	Binary		
8nH	1000nnnn	0kkkkkkk	Note Off
		0vvvvvvv	vvvvvvv: note off velocity
9nH	1001nnnn	0kkkkkkk	Note On
		0vvvvvvv	vvvvvvv ≠ 0: velocity
			vvvvvvv = 0: note off
AnH	1010nnnn	0kkkkkkk	Polyphonic Key Pressure (Aftertouch)
		0vvvvvvv	vvvvvvv: pressure value
BnH	1011nnnn	0ccccccc	Control Change (See Table III)
		0vvvvvvv	ccccccc: control # (0-120)
			vvvvvvv: control value
			ccccccc = 121 thru 127: Reserved. (See Table IV)
CnH	1100nnnn	0ppppppp	Program Change
			ppppppp: program number (0-127)
DnH	1101nnnn	0vvvvvvv	Channel Pressure (Aftertouch)
			vvvvvvv: pressure value
EnH	1110nnnn	0vvvvvvv	Pitch Bend Change LSB
		0vvvvvvv	Pitch Bend Change MSB

NOTES:

1. nnnn: Voice Channel number (1-16, coded as defined in Table I notes)

2. kkkkkkk: note number (0 - 127)

3. vvvvvvv: key velocity
   A logarithmic scale is recommended.

4. Continuous controllers are divided into Most Significant and Least Significant Bytes. If only seven bits of resolution are needed for any particular controllers, only the MSB is sent. It is not necessary to send the LSB. If more resolution is needed, then both are sent, first the MSB, then the LSB. If only the LSB has changed in value, the LSB may be sent without re-sending the MSB.

TABLE III

CONTROLLER NUMBERS

CONTROL NUMBER (2nd Byte value)		CONTROL FUNCTION
Decimal	Hex	
0	00H	Undefined
1	01H	Modulation wheel or lever
2	02H	Breath Controller
3	03H	Undefined
4	04H	Foot controller
5	05H	Portamento time
6	06H	Data entry MSB
7	07H	Main volume
8	08H	Balance
9	09H	Undefined
10	0AH	Pan
11	0BH	Expression Controller
12–15	0C–0FH	Undefined
16–19	10–13H	General Purpose Controllers (#'s 1-4)
20–31	14–1FH	Undefined
32–63	20–3FH	LSB for values 0-31
64	40H	Damper pedal (sustain)
65	41H	Portamento
66	42H	Sostenuto
67	43H	Soft pedal
68	44H	Undefined
69	45H	Hold 2
70–79	46–4FH	Undefined
80–83	50–53H	General Purpose Controllers (#'s 5-8)
84–90	54–5AH	Undefined
91	5BH	External Effects Depth
92	5CH	Tremelo Depth
93	5DH	Chorus Depth
94	5EH	Celeste (Detune) Depth
95	5FH	Phaser Depth
96	60H	Data increment
97	61H	Data decrement
98	62H	Non-Registered Parameter Number LSB
99	63H	Non-Registered Parameter Number MSB
100	64H	Registered Parameter Number LSB
101	65H	Registered Parameter Number MSB
102–120	66–78H	Undefined
121–127	79–7FH	Reserved for Channel Mode Messages

TABLE IIIa

REGISTERED PARAMETER NUMBERS

Parameter Number		Function
LSB	MSB	
00H	00H	Pitch Bend Sensitivity
01H	00H	Fine Tuning
02H	00H	Coarse Tuning

TABLE IV

CHANNEL MODE MESSAGES

STATUS		DATA BYTES	DESCRIPTION
Hex	Binary		
Bn	1011nnnn	0ccccccc 0vvvvvvv	**Mode Messages**
			ccccccc = 121: Reset All Controllers vvvvvvv = 0
			ccccccc = 122:Local Control vvvvvvv = 0, Local Control Off vvvvvvv = 127, Local Control On
			ccccccc = 123: All Notes Off vvvvvvv = 0
			ccccccc = 124: Omni Mode Off (All Notes Off) vvvvvvv = 0
			ccccccc = 125:Omni Mode On (All Notes Off) vvvvvvv = 0
			ccccccc = 126: Mono Mode On (Poly Mode Off) (All Notes Off) vvvvvvv = M, where M is the number of channels. vvvvvvv = 0, the number of channels equals the number of voices in the receiver.
			ccccccc = 127: Poly Mode On (Mono Mode Off) (All Notes Off) vvvvvvv = 0

NOTES:

1. nnnn: Basic Channel number (1-16)

2. ccccccc: Controller number (121 - 127)

3. vvvvvvv: Controller value

TABLE V

SYSTEM COMMON MESSAGES

| STATUS | | DATA BYTES | DESCRIPTION |
Hex	Binary		
F1H	11110001	0nnndddd	MIDI Time Code Quarter Frame nnn: Message Type dddd: Values
F2H	11110010	01111111 0hhhhhhh	Song Position Pointer 1111111: (Least significant) hhhhhh: (Most significant)
F3H	11110011	0sssssss	Song Select sssssss: Song #
F4H	11110100		Undefined
F5H	11110101		Undefined
F6H	11110110	none	Tune Request
F7H	11110111	none	EOX: "End of System Exclusive" flag

TABLE VI

SYSTEM REAL TIME MESSAGES

STATUS		DATA BYTES	DESCRIPTION
Hex	Binary		
F8H	11111000		Timing Clock
F9H	11111001		Undefined
FAH	11111010		Start
FBH	11111011		Continue
FCH	11111100		Stop
FDH	11111101		Undefined
FEH	11111110		Active Sensing
FFH	11111111		System Reset

TABLE VII

SYSTEM EXCLUSIVE MESSAGES

STATUS		DATA BYTES	DESCRIPTION
Hex	Binary		
F0H	11110000		Bulk dump, etc.
		0iiiiiii	iiiiiii: identification (See note 1)
		.	
		(0ddddddd)	
		.	Any number of data bytes may be sent here, for any
		.	purpose, as long as they all have a zero in the most
		.	significant bit.
		(0ddddddd)	
F7H	11110111		EOX: "End of System Exclusive"

NOTES:

1. iiiiiii: identification ID (0-127). If the ID is 0 the following two bytes are used as extensions to the manufacturer ID.

2. All bytes between the System Exclusive Status byte and EOX must have zeroes in the MSB.

3. A manufacturer's ID number can be obtained from the MMA or JMSC.

4. Status or Data bytes (except Real-Time) should not be interleaved with System Exclusive

5. No Status Bytes (other than Real-time) should be sent until after an EOX has terminated the System Exclusive message. If however, a Status Byte other than EOX is received during a System Exclusive message, the message is terminated.

6. Three System Exclusive ID numbers have been set aside for special purposes: 7DH is reserved for non-commercial use (e.g. schools, research, etc.) and is not to be used on any product released to the public; 7EH (Non-Real Time) and 7FH (Real Time) are used for extensions to the MIDI specification.

TABLE VIII

CURRENTLY DEFINED UNIVERSAL SYSTEM EXCLUSIVE ID NUMBERS

SUB-ID #1	SUB-ID #2	DESCRIPTION
Non-Real Time (7EH)		
00	--	**Unused**
01	(not used)	**Sample Dump Header**
02	(not used)	**Sample Data Packet**
03	(not used)	**Sample Dump Request**
04	nn	**MIDI Time Code**
	00	Special
	01	Punch In Points
	02	Punch Out Points
	03	Delete Punch In Point
	04	Delete Punch Out Point
	05	Event Start Point
	06	Event Stop Point
	07	Event Start Points with additional info.
	08	Event Stop Points with additional info.
	09	Delete Event Start Point
	0A	Delete Event Stop Point
	0B	Cue Points
	0C	Cue Points with additional info.
	0D	Delete Cue Point
	0E	Event Name in additional info.
05	nn	**Sample Dump Extensions**
	01	Multiple Loop Points
	02	Loop Points Request
06	nn	**General Information**
	01	Identity Request
	02	Identity Reply
7C	(not used)	**Wait**
7D	(not used)	**Cancel**
7E	(not used)	**NAK**
7F	(not used)	**ACK**
Real Time (7FH)		
00	--	**Unused**
01	nn	**MIDI Time Code**
	01	Full Message
	02	User Bits

NOTES:

1. The standardized format for both Real Time and Non-Real Time messages is as follows: `F0H <id number> <channel number> <sub-ID#1> <sub-ID#2>...... F7H`

TABLE IX

SYSTEM EXCLUSIVE MANUFACTURER'S ID NUMBERS*

NUMBER	MANUFACTURER	NUMBER	MANUFACTURER
			European Group
	American Group		
		20H	Passac
01H	Sequential	21H	SIEL
02H	IDP	22H	Synthaxe
03H	Octave-Plateau	24H	Hohner
04H	Moog	25H	Twister
05H	Passport Designs	26H	Solton
06H	Lexicon	27H	Jellinghaus MS
07H	Kurzweil	28H	Southworth
08H	Fender	29H	PPG
0AH	AKG Acoustics	2AH	JEN
0BH	Voyce Music	2BH	SSL Limited
0CH	Waveframe Corp	2CH	Audio Veritrieb
0DH	ADA	2FH	Elka
0EH	Garfield Elec.	30H	Dynacord
0FH	Ensoniq		
10H	Oberheim		**Japanese Group**
11H	Apple Computer		
12H	Grey Matter Response	40H	Kawai
14H	Palm Tree Inst.	41H	Roland
15H	JL Cooper	42H	Korg
16H	Lowrey	43H	Yamaha
17H	Adams-Smith	44H	Casio
18H	Emu Systems	46H	Kamiya Studio
19H	Harmony Systems	47H	Akai
1AH	ART	48H	Japan Victor
1BH	Baldwin	49H	Meisosha
1CH	Eventide	4AH	Hoshino Gakki
1DH	Inventronics	4BH	Fujitsu Elect
1FH	Clarity	4CH	Sony
		4DH	Nisshin Onpa
00H 00H 07H	Digital Music Corp.	4EH	TEAC Corp.
00H 00H 0BH	IVL Technologies	4FH	System Product
00H 00H 0CH	Southern Music Systems	50H	Matsushita Electric
00H 00H 0DH	Lake Butler Sound	51H	Fostex
00H 00H 10H	DOD Electronics		
00H 00H 14H	Perfect Fretworks		
00H 00H 16H	Opcode		
00H 00H 18H	Spatial Sound		
00H 00H 19H	KMX		
00H 00H 20H	Axxes		

* Current as of June, 1988

Bibliography

Anderton, C., *MIDI For Musicians*. New York: Amsco Publications, 1986. An overview of MIDI, plus details of the MIDI language. Explains MIDI modes, messages, hexadecimal notation, and much more.

Boom, Michael. *Music Through MIDI*. Redmond, VA: Microsoft Press, 1987. An overview of MIDI. An excellent introduction for people who have not worked with MIDI instruments.

Chamberlin, H. *Musical Applications of Microprocessors*. Indianapolis: Hayden Books, 1985. This is a technical overview of all aspects of electronic sound generation and analysis. Analog and digital techniques are discussed in detail, along with analytical techniques such as Fourier analysis and filter theory. The author assumes that the reader is familiar with electronic circuits, but keeps the mathematics fairly simple (little calculus).

Conger, Jim. *C Programming For MIDI*. Redwood City, CA: M&T Books, 1988. Provides an introduction to C programming for MIDI applications.

Feldstein, Sandy. *Drum Machine Rhythm Dictionary*. Van Nuys, CAAlfred Publishing Co., Inc., 1987. Provides a wide range of drum patterns in both musical notation and drum machine format. An excellent starting point for working up a rhythm track.

Garvin, M. "Designing a Music Recorder." *Dr. Dobb's Journal of Software Tools* 127 (May 1987). This is the only article I have seen that addresses sequencer design in detail.

Hancock, Les, and Krieger, Morris, *The C Primer*. New York: McGraw-Hill Inc., 1986. An excellent book to get you started with the C language.

Kernighan, B.W., and Ritchie, D.M. *The C Programming Language, Second Edition*. Englewood Cliffs, NJ: Prentice-Hall, Inc., 1988. The second edition is updated to include the ANSI standard. A must for C programmers.

Norton, P. *Programmer's Guide to the IBM PC*. Bellevue, WA: Microsoft Press, 1985. This book explains how the IBM PC (and related clones) work. All BIOS and DOS calls, interrupt vectors, and screen modes are explained.

Microsoft C Optimizing Compiler User's Guide, Version 5.1. Microsoft Corporation, 1987. These manuals come with the compiler.

MIDI 1.0 Detailed Specification, MIDI Manufacturers Association, 1988. Published and distributed by the International MIDI Association, 5316 W. 57th St., Los Angeles, CA, 90056. This is the detailed technical description of the MIDI communication protocol.

MIDI Processing Unit MPU-401 Technical Reference Manual. Roland Corporation, 1985. This book comes with the MPU-401.

Standard MIDI Files 1.0, MIDI Manufacturers Association, 1988. Published and distributed by the International MIDI Association, 5316 W. 57th St., Los Angeles, CA, 90056. This is the detailed technical description of the MIDI files standard for exchanging sequencer data.

Turbo C User's Guide, Version 2.0. Borland International, 1988. These manuals come with the compiler.

About the Author

Jim Conger's interest in MIDI stems from his background as both a programmer and a musician. He has been programming for eighteen years and has played woodwinds for twenty-five years. MIDI has allowed Jim to merge his two primary interests and to do more, musically, than was ever possible with conventional instruments. Conger is also the author of *C Programming for MIDI* (M&T Books, 1988).

Index

G

g_cursor_attrib   216
g_emph_attrib   143, 216
Genius mouse (GMENU)   29
get401() function   127, 146,
    (MTRC4.C line 81)
getdata() function   127, 214,
    (MIO401.ASM line 81)
getdrive() function   (FILEFUNC.C
    line 120)
get_drive() function   204
getfloat() function   227
get_from_file() function   110, 199,
    206, (FILEFUNC.C line 183)
getint() function   227
getnext401() function   126, 145,
    (MTRC4.C line 64)
getstr() function   229, (INPUTF.C
    line 98)
get_string() function   229,
    (INPUTF.C line 115)
g_file_disp   203
g_norm_attrib   143, 216
g_notes[] data array   109, 119, 161,
    168, 178
GLOBAL   113
global variables   112
goto_measure() function   148,
    (MTRC4.C line 167)
graphics global variables   179, 182
graphics mode (programming)   178
graphics video modes   27
g_trace_on   127, 147, 148
g_trackarray[]   124, 126, 170
g_track_vel_used   138

H

half-steps   71
hard code   119
has_midi_data() function   156,
    163–4, (MTED2.C line 83)
header files   116

help_control() function   209–10,
    (MTUT1.C line 219)
helpdisp() function   210, (MTUT1.C
    line 273)
HELP menu   31
Hercules graphics   27
Hercules graphics mode   218
hex   76
higher octave command   59
hung notes   158

I

implied note offs   246
IMPORT command   65, 67
IMPORT menu   66, 199
import_menu() function   200, 210–
    11, (MTUT2.C line 19)
import track command   67
import_track() function   211
increment_measure() function
    164, (MTED2.C line 114)
init_401() function   128, 138,
    (MTRC3.C line 81)
init_edit_param() function   182,
    (MTSC1.C line 183)
init_meas_data() function 156, 163–
    4, (MTED2.C line 17)
init_note_array() function   161, 168,
    (MTED2.C line 342)
    init_rec_val() function   142,
    (MTRC3.C line 271)
init_screen_box() function
    (MTSC2.C line 27)
initscrn() function   179, 240,
    (WRITSCRN.C line 165)
init_tracks() function   150,
    (MTRC4.C line 222)
init_track_str() function   141,
    (MTRC3.C line 207)
inpchain() function   232, (CHAIN.C
    line 22)
INPUTF.C   115, 298

More MIDI Books from M&T Books

MIDI Programmer's Handbook

by Steve DeFuria and Joe Scacciaferro of Ferro Technologies

The *MIDI Programmer's Handbook* is a complete and indispensible reference for anyone writing MIDI programs. It is the ideal resource for programmers and musicians currently programming MIDI applications. And because it is not specific to any computer system or language it is equally useful to IBM, Atari, Commodore, and Apple programmers. Authors DeFuria and Scacciaferro begin with an overview of MIDI as a communication standard then move on to a detailed investigation of the make-up, contents, and implications of every currently defined MIDI message. Also presented is a look into the different ways MIDI is implemented in commercial devices, with a focus on what programmers can expect to find when writing software to interact with commercial MIDI devices. Finally, the authors present various examples of how to approach specific MIDI related tasks from within a program. Basic and Pascal routines are used to illustrate the concepts and techniques. These routines make up a "toolbox" of MIDI functions that can be transported onto any computer in any language.

Book & Disk (MS-DOS, Macintosh, Atari)   *Item #068-0*   *$39.99*
Book only   *Item #069-9*   *$24.95*
Available OCTOBER 1989

C Programming for MIDI

by Jim Conger

Both musicians and programmers can learn how to create useful programs and libraries of software tools for music applications. Outlined are the features of MIDI and its support of real-time access to musical devices. An introduction to C programming fundamentals as they relate to MIDI is provided. These concepts are fully demonstrated with two MIDI applications: a patch librarian and a simple sequencer. Some of the fundamental MIDI programming elements you'll learn are: full development of a patch librarian program, sequencing applications for the MPU-401 interface, how to create screen displays, and how to write low-level assembly language routines for MIDI. *C Programming for MIDI* shows you how to write customized programs to create the sounds and effects you need. All programs are available on disk with full source code. Supports both Microsoft C and Turbo C.

Book & Disk (MS-DOS)   *Item #90-9*   *$37.95*
Book only   *Item #86-0*   *$22.95*

More MIDI Tools ...

MIDI Programming for the Macintosh

Steve De Furia and Joe Scacciaferro of Ferro Technologies

This book equips musicians and programmers with the background necessary to program music applications and take advantage of all that the Macintosh and MIDI interface have to offer. Authors De Furia and Scacciaferro begin with an excellent introduction to MIDI and Macintosh programming, covering such topics as MIDI devices (hardware and software), the Macintosh user interface, program design, Macintosh programming languages and tools, and MIDI code resources.

The authors then delve into programming applications presenting the basics of programming the Macintosh's ROM-based toolbox and giving the reader a set of software tools that can be used and expanded upon in any Macintosh application. The final sections present guidelines for creating one's own software. All the programs are available on an optional disk with full source code and compiled applications and resource files.

Book & Disk   *Item #022-2 $37.95*
Book   *Item #021-4 $22.95*

MIDI and Sound Book for the Atari ST

Bernd Enders and Wolfgang Klemme

Find out why the Atari ST is one of the hottest MIDI computers available and how to make it work. This book provides you with an introduction to the acoustic and musical basics of sound sythesis and sound chip programming. With a detailed description of MIDI technology, you can learn to utilize MIDI functions to suit your specific needs.

Along with a discussion of commercially marketed samplers, the *MIDI and Sound Book for the Atari ST* contains an assembler routine plus a hardware description of a do-it-yourself 8-bit converter. A GFA-Basic program on the optional disk provides a short introduction to music theory-notes, sounds, keys, and intervals. Other example programs are also included on disk.

Book & Disk (Atari)   *Item #043-5 $34.95*
Book   *Item #042-7 $17.95*

More MIDI Tools ...

MIDI Sequencing in C

Jim Conger

Picking up where his popular book *C Programming for MIDI* left off, Jim Conger's *MIDI Sequencing in C* approaches the recording and playback of MIDI data from the perspective of both users and programmers. The first few chapters provide a tutorial, describing the multi-track sequencer from the user's point of view. The remaining chapters describe how the program works. Covered are such topics as program documenation, higher-level video functions, the multi-track eight-track MIDI recorder, measure level editing functions, note level editing, and file and utility functions.

The optional disk is highly recommended. For the non-programmer there is a ready-to-use eight-track MIDI sequencer with editing features. For the developing programmer the source code for the multi-track sequencer follows the programming examples in *C Programming for MIDI* and expands them into a full application. This can serve as a starting point for experiments and additions to the basic MT program. For the experienced programmer, the source code provides functions that can be applied to a wide range of MIDI projects.

The program will run on IBM PCs, ATs, or equivalent computers using the Roland MPU-401 MIDI interface (or equivalent).

Book & Disk   *Item #046-X*   *$39.95*
Book   *Item #045-1*   *$24.95*

To Order: Return this form with your payment to **M&T Books**, 501 Galveston Drive, Redwood City, CA 94063 or **CALL TOLL-FREE 1-800-533-4372** Mon-Fri 8AM-5PM Pacific Standard Time (in California, call 1-800-356-2002).

☐ **YES!** Please send me the following: ☐ Check enclosed, payable to **M&T Books**.

Item#	Description	Disk	Price

Charge my ☐ Visa ☐ MC ☐ AmEx

Card No. _____ Exp. Date _____

Signature _____

Name _____

Address _____

City _____

State _____ Zip _____

Subtotal _____

CA residents add sales tax __ % _____

Add $2.99 per item for shipping _____

TOTAL _____

Disk Format: ☐ MS-DOS ☐ Macintosh ☐ Atari

7023

M&T BOOKS